Day Trading:

The Ultimate Beginner's Guide

Lee Maxwell

© 2016

© **Copyright 2016 by Lee Maxwell - All rights reserved.**

This document is geared towards providing exact and reliable information in regards to the topic and issue covered. The publication is sold with the idea that the publisher is not required to render accounting, officially permitted, or otherwise, qualified services. If advice is necessary, legal or professional, a practiced individual in the profession should be ordered.

- From a Declaration of Principles which was accepted and approved equally by a Committee of the American Bar Association and a Committee of Publishers and Associations.

In no way is it legal to reproduce, duplicate, or transmit any part of this document in either electronic means or in printed format. Recording of this publication is strictly prohibited and any storage of this document is not allowed unless with written permission from the publisher. All rights reserved.

The information provided herein is stated to be truthful and consistent, in that any liability, in terms of inattention or otherwise, by any usage or abuse of any policies, processes, or directions contained within is the solitary and utter responsibility of the recipient reader. Under no circumstances will any legal responsibility or blame be held against the publisher for any reparation, damages, or monetary loss due to the information herein, either directly or indirectly.

Respective authors own all copyrights not held by the publisher.

The information herein is offered for informational purposes solely, and is universal as so. The presentation of the information is without contract or any type of guarantee assurance.

The trademarks that are used are without any consent, and the publication of the trademark is without permission or backing by the trademark owner. All trademarks and brands within this book are for clarifying purposes only and are the owned by the owners themselves, not affiliated with this document.

Disclaimer and Terms of Use: The Author and Publisher has strived to be as accurate and complete as possible in the creation of this book, notwithstanding the fact that he does not warrant or represent at any time that the contents within are accurate due to the rapidly changing nature of the Internet. While all attempts have been made to verify information provided in this publication, the Author and Publisher assumes no responsibility for errors, omissions, or contrary interpretation of the subject matter herein. Any perceived slights of specific persons, peoples, or organizations are unintentional. In practical advice books, like anything else in life, there are no guarantees of results. Readers are cautioned to rely on their own judgment about their individual circumstances and act accordingly. This book is not intended for use as a source of legal, medical, business, accounting or financial advice. All readers are advised to seek services of competent professionals in the legal, medical, business, accounting, and finance fields.

TABLE OF CONTENT

1. Day Trading Stocks Practice

2. Some Rules to Online Day Trading

3. What Are Day Trading and Swing Trading? What's the Difference?

4. The Basics Of Day Trading

5. How to choose shares (stocks) for day trading

6. Conclusion

Introduction

I want to thank you and congratulate you for downloading the book, "Day trading: The Ultimate Beginner's Guide".

This book contains proven steps and strategies on how Day Trading works...

Indicator Only Day Trader - Setup Including Indicators Method Day Trader

I have attempted to discuss the way I started day trading, and the way I think many-most traders typically begin. Along with this, I have pointed various issues and problems that I had - those regarding how to learn to trade, and then progressing into a profitable trader. My experiences have been both personal, as well as those of many traders that I have worked with over the last 8-9 years through Tactical Trading - that a very large number of these problems are due to day trading only with indicators, the specific indicators used, along with trying to turn these indicators into a mechanical trading system. This is not to say that this can't be done - I simply couldn't do it.

However, I would strongly suggest that anyone who is in the early stages of day trading, or struggling with their day trading, consider these things that have been discussed.

There is no shortage of advice available about what we should do. That is O.K. and it is necessary, but it is not enough by itself. For balance we should also understand the other side of this. We have to determine what to keep from doing and what to avoid.

This article can help you with how to to open day trading stocks practice. It helps not by telling you what you should do. It can help by teaching you five things you will want to avoid if you want to to open day trading stocks practice, as well as, understanding how you can study all of the day trade indicators, signals, setups, triggers and tips-offs to enter a trade and manage the trade for earnings. There's a reason the professionals know when you should get into a trade and how to manage the trade. Intra-day trading can be mastered, but That said, here are the 5 things you should avoid:

1. If Not 100% Confident In Your Trade, Do Not Enter If You Want To To Open A Day Trading Stocks Practice!

There are particular reasons to refrain from doing this. The main one is If your not confident whenever you enter the trade, next time around you will feel this same insecurity, but most likely amplified. You'll create a hard habit to get rid of. Trading with fear isn't fun. Confidence originates from being prepared. You have to do your homework and also you should be prepared should you ever intend to to open day trading stocks practice. Preparation includes: pre-market homework, knowing where your entry points will occur before the trade sets up and following your pre-determined and written rules. You have to have rules in place. A lot better alternative could be to have rules in place which leads me to point number 2.

2. Do Not Trade Real Money Without Training If You Want To Open A Day Trading Stocks Practice!

The reason for this is because trading without correct training is suicide. I don't mean training as in you have a buddy provide you with a book or simply reading information online. Instead, you could simply In life, we usually receive what we put into something. Should you treat daytrading just like a hobby, you'll get hobby results, if your lucky. Daytrading doesn't have remorse and can rob you blind. Buy a course which has live daytrading examples and shows live trade setups and when they occur should you ever plan to open day trading stocks practice.

Thanks again for downloading this book, I hope you enjoy it!

Chapter 1

Day Trading Stocks Practice

5 Things To Avoid When Opening Day Trading Stocks Practice

There is no shortage of advice available about what we should do. That is O.K. and it is necessary, but it is not enough by itself. For balance we should also understand the other side of this. We have to determine what to keep from doing and what to avoid.

This article can help you with how to to open day trading stocks practice. It helps not by telling you what you should do. It can help by teaching you five things you will want to avoid if you want to to open day trading stocks practice, as well as, understanding how you can study all of the day trade indicators, signals, setups, triggers and tips-offs to enter a trade and manage the trade for earnings. There's a reason the professionals know when you should get into a trade and how to manage the trade. Intra-day trading can be mastered, but That said, here are the 5 things you should avoid:

1. If Not 100% Confident In Your Trade, Do Not Enter If You Want To To Open A Day Trading Stocks Practice!

There are particular reasons to refrain from doing this. The main one is If your not confident whenever you enter the trade, next time around you will feel this same insecurity, but most likely amplified. You'll create a hard habit to get rid of. Trading with fear isn't fun. Confidence originates from being prepared. You have to do your homework and also you should be prepared should you ever intend to to open day trading stocks practice. Preparation includes: pre-market homework, knowing where your entry points will occur before the trade sets up and following your pre-determined and written rules. You have to have rules in place. A lot better alternative could be to have rules in place which leads me to point number 2.

2. Do Not Trade Real Money Without Training If You Want To Open A Day Trading Stocks Practice!

The reason for this is because trading without correct training is suicide. I don't mean training as in you have a buddy provide you with a book or simply reading information online. Instead, you could simply In life, we usually receive what we put into something. Should you treat daytrading just like a hobby, you'll get hobby results, if your lucky. Daytrading doesn't have remorse and can rob you blind. Buy a course which has live daytrading examples and shows live trade setups and when they occur should you ever plan to open day trading stocks practice.

3. If Planning to To Open A Day Trading Stocks Practice Do Not Study Static Charts Alone!

Do not buy a course that only shows charts in books or spread sheets. I could teach you in an hour when and how to enter a trade by only considering candle stick patterns on a static chart, a 4 year old boy could let you know this. And what you would like to do instead is look for a course, such as the Day Trading Template and Training Course, which has real live trade examples if you ever plan to open day trading stocks practice. There are many factors that are involved when taking trades and candle stick patterns aren't the only indicator. The truth is, you should be studying the Market Profile, Time & Sales, Tick & Trin, a Tick Chart, a Simple Moving Average- on different time frames, MACD, long time-frame charts and more immediate time-frame charts. The market is unforgiving, a lot of the courses today put to much emphasis on candle stick patterns and hold trades to long. This leads me to number 4 which is:

4. Entering A Trade Without A Proper Stop Loss in Place Is Suicide. Do Not Do It If You Want To Open A Day Trading Stocks Practice!

The primary reason why this is a blunder is stop losses are in place is so that you don't blow up your whole trade account in one or two day trades. If your planning to open day trading stocks practice, you have to discover how to enter trades with short stop losses and good money management. Good money management is a must for successful trading. The Day Trading Templates and Training Course uses a 4-6 tick stop loss. This is unheard of inside the stock investing industry. Most hold positions overnight or go thousands in the red before entering the black. That is to much risk, in my opinion. Why hold a trade thousands of dollars into the red? Trading in that fashion is much like rolling the dice, hoping and praying it turns in your direction. As a matter of fact, you'll probably have better odds at a casino. Instead you really ought to enter a trade exactly once the market is headed in the direction you want, given all indicators line up. One does this by understanding proper trading principals and entering trades with commercial paper. Commercial paper are big lot traders like Goldman Sachs and Merrill Lynch. These big players know where the market is headed and when the market is headed there. This leads me to the thing to avoid:

5. Never Follow Floor Traders, Follow Commercial Paper If You Want To Open A Day Trading Stocks Practice!

Don't ever do this for long because Floor Traders are scalpers. Floor traders scalp 2-4 ticks in most cases bail a trade. They're much more experienced than most traders and push industry from both sides of the Market Profile. Their goal is to push the marketplace towards the high or low of day, usually the Market Profile VAH (value area high) or VAL (value area low) to locate initiating activity. Initiating activity is large commercial paper that steps in the market and brings large momentum moves for local traders to ride. Should you to open day trading stocks practice, never follow floor traders, no matter how good or mouth watering the trade looks. Do not forget that the commercial traders are those that make the marketplace move. Watch the time and sales and look for big lots of 50 to enter the marketplace. If all other indicators match up and commercial paper steps in the market, you could have yourself a winner.

Be certain to avoid all 5 of the things mentioned and your chances to to open day trading stocks practice are greatly increased!

Day Trading Secrets Exposed - The 5 Great Myths of Day Trading Explained and Exposed

Day trading has become a popular vehicle for (attempting to) create or maintain wealth. Every single day, thousands of new Day Traders emerge from the sidelines, primed and ready for action. They eagerly seek to learn day trading success strategies used by the Master Traders.

However, when a new or a struggling day trader begins to investigate and explore the world of Trading, in an effort to make their own dramatic entrance or to improve on their results, they are confronted by a world full of seemingly insurmountable challenges and obstacles.

But these new and/or struggling Traders don't realize that MOST of these obstacles are myths.

And because they fail to recognize this, these new or struggling Traders typically fall prey to one of the 5 Great Myths of Trading:

1. Day Trading always requires massive capital accounts, both to learn, and then to execute a Day Trading Strategy.

It is true that in many cases you do need massive capital up front in order to step into the Trading arena, depending on where you learn trading, and what investment vehicle you choose to trade. But it certainly doesn't HAVE to be.

In fact, it's possible to secure an excellent Trading education AND fund a trading account with as little as $3000.

This is a little known fact among newbie Traders - they assume they'll need to have at least $25,000 to open a trading account, on top of the $10,000+ they paid an "expert" to learn a trading system.

2. Day Trading always requires countless hours spent chained to your computer, staring at stock charts.

The stereotype of a Day Trader is someone who spends ALL DAY LONG glued to their computer screens, staring at stock charts, waiting for indicators to tell them its time to make a move.

And in large part, this stereotype is justified, because this is true of most Traders. These Day Traders will literally spend HOURS, if not ALL DAY LONG at their computers trading.

They use Trading as a means to escape the corporate rat race... only to find themselves in a J-O-B of their own creation.

But it doesn't have to be this way. In fact, it is entirely possible to be an incredibly efficient and successful Trader while trading for just a few minutes a day - if you know how.

3. It takes months (or even longer) to learn and fully grasp a "successful" day trading strategy

Like the other myths, this one CAN be true, and IS true of many (most?) traders. The reason for this is most traders use technical trading systems and strategies.

The primary problem with these technically strategies is actually the topic of Myth #4 (to follow) - but suffice it to say that technical trading systems will take months to learn, and involved hundreds if not THOUSANDS of "practice trades" before you can possibly be ready to start trading "live" (i.e. with real money).

And when you DO go "live", that doesn't mean that you've fully grasped the trading strategy. In fact, it will be months or even years after going "live" before you likely have a firm handle on your technical trading strategy or system.

But like the other Great Trading Myths, it doesn't HAVE to be this way.

In fact, it is possible to learn certain trading strategies and be ready to successfully implement them in a matter of weeks, or even DAYS.

If you know what these ultra-efficient strategies are, and where to find them.

4. You need a PhD in Advanced Statistical Theory in order to trade successfully.

This myth is a little bit "tongue in cheek", but you no doubt understand the concept here. Many day traders typically employ a Technical trading style, which involved the use of statistical probability formulas and other highly complex technical indicators.

New traders see the level of complexity often involved with technical trading or "trend trading", and are so intimidated by it that it keeps them from ever trying learn day trading.

Also, most people who try to learn technical analysis will struggle and eventually fail, because it IS so complex, and the technical indicators can often be very ambiguous.

The extreme complexity of technical trading systems may be the single biggest factor that prevents new traders from entering the Trading Arena.

5. You don't need to learn how to trade from a professional - you can just teach yourself.

Of all of the 5 Great Trading Myths, this one runs the most rampant, and is responsible for destroying the overwhelming majority of trading accounts.

If there is one thing that new Traders need to understand, and that struggling or failed Traders understand all to well, it's this:

You are going to have to pay for your trading education, one way or another. You can either pay to learn how to trade from a Professional, OR you can pay the Market.

And the market is a much more cruel, and a much more expensive instructor than nearly any Trading professional that will teach you how to trade.

Those Traders who want to try to "figure out how to trade" all on their own, with maybe the help of a book or two, will quickly discover that this is absolutely true.

The Market loves to dine on the trading accounts of inexperienced and uneducated day traders. Don't let YOUR trading account become an afternoon snack for the Market.

When you are finally ready to learn day trading, explore the various options available to you before settling on any specific day trading system or strategy.

Chapter 2

Some Rules to Online Day Trading

A day trader is one trading stocks, options, commodities, or futures on the web. Many times new day traders ask the difference between stock/options trading vs. futures day trading. This question comes up many times in our user's camp. Now, if the rules are overlooked unintentionally (or knowingly), let's discuss what they are and what happens if violated.

This article only debates online day trading as it relates for stocks and options vs commodities and futures. Commodities and Futures have similar online day trading rules.

If you have been part of trading for any time, I'm sure you have heard of the 431 Rule. It is defined as a (Margin requirement) for any customer who performs four or more same online day trades inside any five successive business days. Further, your online day trading activities are greater than six percent of your total trading activity for that same 5 day period (from FINRA site). Having a margin call is no fun and must be answered if violated. As a day trader trading stocks are options with less than $25,000 in your account, you must be aware of trading this money more than 1 time in the 5 day period.

Day trading futures and commodities does not have this type of margin requirement. Margin requirements when day trading differ in you can make multiple trades in a given day and there are no limits to how frequently you can trade your money.

Rules for a Online Trading

The equity in your trading account must be retained over $25,000 to be in a position to trade and not run into issues. If not, say you trade $5,000 and cash out of your position within 10 min. That $5,000 can not be traded for 5 days. Strange rule I know, but that is the rule.

Trading futures and commodities, margins can be as low as $500 and once cashed out of a position, the same money can be traded again with no wait time.

Only three trades in a week (5 trading days) are permitted or you'll be given a 90-day suspension of all trading activities if you still engage in trade on the 4th day.

A day trader can transact many times in a day with no limitations.

Hence, in my opinion, day trading is a better path to take if your taking multiple trades in a day.

When stock trading the amount of $25,000 equity should be maintained in your trading account. During buying and selling similar stock/option in the same day, do not go into a new trade where the funds from the sale of the stock just sold will be used to acquire a new position. If you have purchased a position from cash from a previous same day sell, it is best to save that position overnight.

The trading rules I have offered here are the ones I have run across through all the years i have been doing trade. You can get all-encompassing info by exploring the online network for online day trading and pattern day trader. Wikipedia can be utilized to get such info.

I have traded a number of years in accounts with less than $25k and have never had a 90-day suspension canon applied, but have had more than a few alerts about a trade that will prompt the ninety-suspension canon. When this takes place, I just do not perform the trade and will pause till next day. Good luck in your trading...

Dispelling the Myths of Day-Trading

As a trader that utilizes both short-term and day-trading strategies, I have been given a unique insight into the true benefits and disadvantages of both. As a teacher of trading, I have also had the opportunity to hear many oft quoted expressions in regard to trading that are firmly believed, but simply do not hold up under scrutiny. Many of these center on the subject of day-trading. If you are interested in day-trading, then it behooves you to know what is true and what is not.

Myth 1 - Day-trading is risky, much more than short-term trading or investing.

Without doubt, the risk is greater for short-term trading. In any single trade you are risking far less in a day-trade than in ether a short-term trade or long-term investment. What gives the appearance of greater risk is that you are typically taking more trades. Even on my worse day I have never lost as much as I have short-term trading. Yes, that is right. Even on my worse day combining all of those day trades I still have not matched what I have lost with some of my short-term trades even though they are just one single trade. My own experience demonstrates that short-term trading and investing often proves riskier than day-trading. Surprised? You shouldn't be, it is a matter of common sense. How much do you risk on a day trade as opposed to a short term trade? If a short-term trade has so much of a greater potential loss than any day trade what is going to be the naturally outcome when trades go bad?

Myth 2 - Day-trading is gambling

Any trading is gambling if you trade without a plan or allow emotion to control your decisions. The key difference is whether you are putting the odds in your favor or not. If you are doing so then the trading, whether you are talking about short-term, investing, or day-trading, becomes a business. If you can't put the odds in your favor then all of them can be considered gambling. None have an advantage over another.

Myth 3 - Day-trading ties you to a computer all day

I have to laugh at this myth. My typical day is an hour and a half in the morning and two hours in the afternoon, with a two hour lunch break. Even when I am trading I don't watch the market all the time because I am waiting for set ups to develop, so often I am playing a game on the computer or watching television while waiting. There are limited times when a market trends during the day, the most profitable times to trade. Most of the time it just consolidates. During these down times when the market is in consolidation there is no need to watch the markets like a hawk. There are very simple ways to alert you when it is time to prepare for a trade. Frequent breaks should be the norm, not the rarity. I don't know of any other career that can pay you as much and yet give you so much free time.

Myth 4 - Day-trading is too stressful

Any trading is stressful if you are losing money, just as any trading is easy if you are making lots of profit. It isn't the type of trading, but how well you adapt to it and whether you are successful or not. The stress of day-trading typically results from two things; poor trading and the inability to adjust emotionally to the fast pace. Day-trading requires much faster responses because they are made in real time. There isn't much time to analyze and then reanalyze a situation before making a decision like a person might do with short-term trades. So a trader needs to know their trading method well, to the point that it is almost second nature and they also need to keep their emotions in check. While it may be difficult to initially do this, many of us have already mastered other endeavors that require real time critical decisions, such as driving an automobile. To acquire such ability is a simply matter of practice, practice and then more practice.

Myth 5 - The Biggest money is made on longer term moves lasting weeks or longer

A day-trader can double, triple, quadruple, and more beyond that of a person trading the longer term trend. This is because a market will naturally weave up and down as it develops, allowing for repeated profits covering the very same range. Having done both I know firsthand that a successful day-trader can blow away any short-term or long term investor when it comes to profits. The only time a short-term trader will manage to make more profit is when a market gaps overnight, but even with this figured in a successful day-trader will usually be rewarded much more handsomely over the long term.

Myth 6 - When you day trade you miss out on the big profits generated by overnight gaps

You also miss out on the overnight losses as well. Gaps indicate high volatility and in many cases the market will swing violently both ways. Day-trading protects you from that overnight risk. But here is the surprising twist about overnight gaps; it is not uncommon for a market to close an overnight gap during the day, giving a day trader a chance to capture the profit generated by overnight trading anyway. There are of course some markets that are not well suited for day-trading, while others are. So market choice can make a considerable difference when it comes to this issue. Trading a market that is inclined to overlap itself during the day will more than make up for any overnight gaps that occur.

While there are many more myths that could be dispelled here, it is also important to be balanced and consider the other side of the coin; the negative aspect of day-trading. While day-trading is a great way to make a living when you are consistently profitable, it can also be the worse career choice if you consistently lose. This is true of any type of trading, but in day-trading an individual typically has given up a regular job and of course, a regular income. Also, more is demanded emotionally. This latter factor is one that most assume is personally of no concern and yet often proves to be the one issue preventing their success. There is an inherent weakness of emotion that everyone has and yet most refuse to believe they personally could have an issue with it. So they often fail to ever address it correctly and it continues to plague them.

However, if a trader does learn to trade profitably on a consistent basis and they also learn to control their emotions then day-trading is absolutely one of the greatest means for making a living that anyone can pursue. The freedom to work when you want to, the amount of money that can be made, and the lifestyle it provides is truly amazing. It really is all that is promised; the dream job. Although it takes a lot of work to reach that goal, do not be swayed by the myths about day-trading. This one is for real.

Chapter 3

What Are Day Trading and Swing Trading? What's the Difference?

Day trading or swing trading refers to the practice of buying and selling multiple stocks within a single day. It is the perfect vehicle for the short term intra-day type trader, who would like to hold on to a position for a short time, a few minutes or a few hour, and squares their positions prior to the end of the day.

Day Trading

The stock or futures day trader is someone who is making trades intraday. They tend to do this with frequency throughout the day. A day trader may trade a few times per day or dozens of times per day.

Swing Trading

The swing trader could be a stock, option or futures investor. This type of trader is looking to take strategic bites out of the stock market that can stretch over a day or multiple days and weeks.

Long Term Swing Trading

The long term swing trader is very much like the regular swing trader, the only difference is their focus is on weeks and months as opposed to normal swing traders who focus on singular days.

Day and swing trading involve taking a position in the markets with a goal of squaring that position before the end of that day.

A day trader typically trades several times a day looking for fractions of a point to a few points per trade, but who close out all their positions by the end of the business day.

A swing Trader has slower cycle of trades, meaning less trades to make, therefore fewer commissions, but also less chance of mistakes and an increased ability to "snag" the more significant multi-day profitable swing trades.

The goal of a day or swing trader is to capitalize on the price movement within a market trading day.

Unlike investors, a day trader may hold positions for only a few seconds or minutes, and never, ever overnight.

What Day Trading really means?

"Day trading " is a widely misused and misunderstood phrase or term. Officially day trading means to not hold on to your stock positions longer than the current trading day; simply put, not holding any stock position overnight. this is really the safest way to day trade, because you are not exposed to any of the potential losses that can occur, while the stock market is closed due to news that could affect the prices of your stocks. Unfortunately, a huge percentage of people who claim to be "day trading" hold stock positions overnight because of fear or greed, thus setting themselves up for the loss or decreasing of their capital. With the fluctuation of trading currencies, the term "day trading" changes a little bit. Since currencies can be traded around the clock, 24-hours-a-day, there is no such thing as "overnight" trading. So you can have open stock positions for longer than a day with active stop losses that could be activated at any time.

Day trading has been divided into a few distinct styles, including:

Scalpers: This particular style of day trading uses the rapid and repeated buying and selling of a large volume of stocks within seconds, minutes or hours. The goal is to earn a small profit share on each transaction while minimizing the risk.

Momentum Traders: This particular style of trading involves identifying and trading stocks that are in a moving pattern during the day, the goal of this type of day trading style is to buy such stocks at bottoms and sell at the tops.

Advantages of Day Trading

No Overnight Risk: Since positions are closed prior to the end of the trading day, news and events that effect next trading day's opening prices do not effect your portfolio or your capital, you have what you had at market close the previous day.

Better Leverage: Day traders have better leverage on their trading capital because of the low margin requirements as their traders that are closed in the same market day. This increased leverage could increase your profits if used correctly.

Ability to profit regardless of Market Direction: Day trading often will utilize short - selling trading to take advantage of declining stock prices. The ability to lock in profits even as market falls throughout the trading day is extremely useful during bear market condition.

Many people think day trading software and robots are illegal but in reality they are perfectly legal and a vital tool for most day or swing traders. I personally use Day Trading Robot because it is the best for swing trading. Most software trading robots are not designed for the many styles of trading outlined in this article only for day trading in general.

Thousands a Day - Day Trading Stock

Day trading stock, at this level of profitability, is obviously unique.

Unlike other individual financial instruments traded, there are thousands of stocks to choose from, any one of which can provide day trading opportunities (otherwise known as big money wins) -

any trading day, at any time of the trading day.

This makes stock day trading exciting, and for those who know how, extremely rewarding. For those who master the new stock day trading game with a coach in a winner's stock trading room, the opportunities for learning, not just stock trading, and wealth building are unlimited.

What is the big payoff that everyone seeks?

To become a successful day trader, with profitable business performance, where they can make thousands a day, any trading day.

What's required to generate this kind of money in the stock trading business?

Of all the success factors, it comes down to three key elements:

First, you must stop trading on your own and start trading with a world-class stock trading coach (like a world-class tennis player learning and performing with a coach to get to and stay at the top of the game)

Second, you need to be playing (trading) a winner's game (system) that your coach recommends, not an old-school game, but a stock trading game big money winners play

Third, you need to gain the confidence, competence, and performance results consistent with those of a stock trading winner, again, facilitated with your own personal coach at your side.

Here's a look at one aspect of stock day trading, from a winner's perspective.

While day trading, it's the job of the winning day trader to find stock trading setups - stocks that present opportunities to make substantial money - what we refer to as stocks in a "tension" state.

A stock in a tension state is simply a stock with an intraday price movement substantially away from its price balance price or the price at yesterday's close, technically speaking, when you view stock trading charts.

Viewing a stock in a tension state would be much like viewing a pendulum with the ball pulled far away from neutral enough that, when released, it's movement tends to accelerate toward its neutral position and beyond.

Stocks, like the pendulum ball, tend to seek a balanced state as well and like the ball, they return to balance and beyond, and then fluctuate above and/or below a neutral price as they eventually return to a state of neutrality, balance, or non-tension state - above, below, or close to the point of beginning, price wise.

This is the price action winning stock traders live for and thrive on, day by trading day.

This new-school trading makes winners feel both fulfilled and alive. Let's take a look.

The winner's focus is to trade this action to win (not the money involved) one or more trades during the trading day - that can generate $500 to $2,000 and more per trade, depending on lot size (the number of stock shares traded). This form of trading to win, that is, absent the focus on the money while trading, is not to be confused with gambling which is what losers love to do at Las Vegas and while day trading stock or any other financial instruments.

Trading on your own, without a coach, using any of the hundreds of old-school, gambler's stock trading systems, lacking stock day trading confidence, competence, and a history of success while day trading is precisely why we say that 98% of all traders are losers - not profitable and otherwise dissatisfied traders.

Thus, only 2% of traders worldwide fall into that category of day trader - winners, consistently profitable winners.

Winners own the game - the rules, the software (with algorithms reflective of losing trader knowledge and trade execution patterns), when they make markets and stock prices move the most.

We designed our game to ride the coat tails of the 2% (who are intent on "killing" the crowd, the 98%), for our fair share of the action.

So, there are three games being played in the stock market, options, commodity, Forex, or any other markets: the winner's game, the loser's game, and our game. (We only trade stocks.)

Day trading stock this way, we find, is a far more interesting and relatively stress free approach to the day trading losers are accustomed to experiencing.

Stock day trading involves the performance of an individual company or companies, many times with familiar products and services exchanged locally and globally, in many instances involving companies managed by recognized leaders in their field.

Both technical and fundamental data influence stock investors, swing traders, and day traders execution decisions.

Each stock has both a technical (long and short-term price action history - charts) and a fundamental (financial performance - balance sheet, profit and loss statements, and earnings histories). This opportunity to trade the price action on any of thousands of stocks, any trading day, and time of the trading day, makes trading stocks far more interesting, and frequently more challenging than other form of day trading.

So, what we do as stock day traders is far more interesting, exciting, and very financially rewarding.

Our system is also **q**uite simple as we only focus on only 20% of what losers watch, trade a fraction of the time and thus experience a fraction of the trading stress, and as such, we have the energy to trade well when opportunities present themselves.

The game has changed, so have we, and so can you - should you qualify.

Chapter 4

The Basics Of Day Trading

Day trading, as the name suggests, means trading-buying and selling-the stocks on the same trading day. The trading positions, usually though not always, are closed before the market closes for the trading day.

Day trading is different from after- hours trading where the trading activity continues even after the regular marketing hours when the stock exchange closes.

Sellers and buyers who participate in day trading are called day traders. Although day trading evokes the image of a hectic trading activity in course of the trading day, it may not be so in actual practice. You may make several trades, say a dozen, in course of a trading day, or, you may limit yourself to just one trade.

You may, in some cases, just buy a stock on one day and sell it on the next day, if you think that selling it on the same day would not prove profitable. There is no legal restriction such as that you must finish off your trading activity the same day. You may, at the most, have to pay some differential on brokerage if you carry your trade to the next day.

In standard practice, traders usually tend to close their trading positions by the end of the same trading day. In any case your trading frequency depends entirely on your trading strategy for that particular day, or, your general trading style and outlook.

There are traders who focus on very short or short term trading. They finish off their trades in a matter of few minutes or even seconds. Such traders buy and sell several times a day and usually their trades consist of high volumes. They are the favorites of the brokers who reward them with big discounts on commissions.

Some traders, however, do not hanker after reduced brokerages. They focus on momentum or trends of the stock movement. They are very patient during their wait for a strong move, which may occur during the trading day. Obviously such day traders make only a few trades.

There are traders who prefer to sell off their stocks before the close of the market day to avoid the risks arising out of the price gaps between the closing price on the day they bought a stock and its opening price on the next day. They consider this practice as a golden rule and follow it almost religiously.

Other traders believe in allowing the profits to run so they stay with the position even after the market closes.

As said earlier, the number of trades you make on a trading day depends upon your trading style or trading strategies.

Profits and risks in day trading

Day traders make quick bucks and also quick losses in a matter of minutes or at the end of the trading day. Day trading may evoke the visions of gamblers gaming in casinos. There is, however, a marked difference between day trading and gambling.

While, you cannot make any calculated moves or devise any intelligent strategies in gambling, except when you are out to cheat others, day trading involves very serious understanding of the process of trading.

You study the general market trends and the movement of the stocks. You make fundamental and technical analysis and keep yourself abreast of the latest news flashes about the stocks of the companies that you trade in and much more.

Day trading is not playing a blind man's buff or just throwing away a dice. You have to be very alert and cautious before every move. It would, therefore, be unfair to call day traders gamblers or bandits as some frustrated losers in day trading are apt to do.

Experienced and intuitive traders generate huge percentage of returns from day trading. Some stock traders manage to mint millions per year solely on the day trading. A large number of persons have successfully made day trading a sole avenue of making their livelihood.

This, however, is not to deny the risks of huge losses in day trading. Those who trade without a calculated and intelligent strategy and discipline are more likely to incur huge losses in day trading. This happens more with those who use borrowed funds, a practice known as buying on margins. They have to pay back the borrowed amounts with huge interests and other penalties if fail to make profits. This is what makes day trading really risky.

Day Trading Training - Secrets, Precautions, Necessities, Tips, And Points To Remember

What is day trading and its advantages?

Day trading-Buying and selling of shares on daily basis is called day trading this is also called as Intra day trading. Whatever you buy today you have to sell it today OR whatever you sell today you have to buy it today and very importantly during market hours that is 9.55 am to 3.30 pm (Indian time).

Advantages of Day Trading -

a) Margin trading - In Day trading you get margin on your balance amount means you get more leverages (amount) on your available balance amount to do day trading this concept is called margin trading. Margin trading is only possible in day trading and not in delivery trading. How much extra amount (margin) you are going to get that totally depends on your broker, or your online system brokers. Some broker provides 3, 4, 5, and 6 times extra margin. If you do margin then you have to square off your open trades on the same day (means if you bought shares then you have to sell and if you sold shares then you have to buy)before market time (that is 3:30 PM) finishes.b) Second important advantage is that you have to pay is less brokerage (commissions) on day trading (Intraday) as compared to delivery trading. This brokerage again depends from broker to broker (or on your online trading system). c) In day trading you can sell and then buy this is called short sell which you cant do in delivery trading. You can sell shares when prices are falling and then buy when price falls further.

Disadvantage of Day Trading

a) As you are benefited to get more extra amount to trade (that is margin trading) and get more extra profit it is also equally true that you are also taking more risk of loss.b) At any cost you have to square off the open transaction before 3:30 PM (especially if you are doing margin trading) at that time the price may not be in your favor.

Basic Requirements for Day trading

A successful day trader or share market trading requires couple of disciplines and following requirements -

1) PC with internet - If you need to do it yourself then you need to have a PC or else you can do it in internet café also. A PC with good internet connection speed. The internet connection should not be slow or should not face any other problem especially in Day Trading.

2) Online Account (Demat Account) - You need to open online share trading account with any of the available banks or online brokers.Points to remember while opening online accounta) Make multiple enquiries and try get low brokerage trading and demat account.b) Also discuss about the margin they provide for day

trading. c) Discuss about fund transfer. The fund transfer should be reliable and easy. Fund transfer from your bank account to account and visa versa. Some online share accounts have integrated savings account which makes easy for you to transfer funds from your saving account to trading account. d) Very important is about service they provide, the research calls, intraday or daily tips. e) Also enquire about their services charges and any other hidden charges if any. f) And also see how reliable and easy is to contact them in case if any emergency. Emergency closing or squaring off trades in case of any technical or other problems

Chapter 5

How to choose shares (stocks) for day trading

In day trading, traders mostly wish to do buying and selling on small profits or else they look for overbought or oversold shares. Taking into consideration these important points following basic things you should look in for shares while choosing them for day trading.- Price Volatility- Volume (quantity)What exactly these terms mean and how to use them while Day Trading.

Price Volatility - The Price volatility means the movement (up and down) of share price should be more (or high) through out the day. In other words the fluctuation in share prices should be on high rate so that it will be easy for you to buy and sell on different prices. Suppose if share is moving up and down in very narrow range then on what price you will buy and sell? So it is always better if you choose shares which have high volatility in price movement.Do you want to know how to find out the high volatility shares then please click here?

Volume (**q**uantity) - Volume means trading **q**uantities. The shares which you choose for day trading should have high volumes (or high traded **q**uantity).Why this is required?The high volume indicates that there is more liquidity. Li**q**uidity means lots of transactions had took place on this share and more people are interested to trade in this share. This will ease your trading job because you will get more exposure to the price to buy and sell at anytime. Due to high volumes there will be also high price fluctuations.

Points to remember for day tradingFollowing are very important points to be always remember by day traders.Entry & exit points, stop loss limits, profit targets, your desired risk/reward profile,amount of capital to be committed to trades, how long you need to hold the share if incase it is against your favor.

Why it is required to practice day trading before starting actual day trading?

It's important to do practice or paper trading before you starts actual trading. Following are the few reasons, 1) Very importantly you will come to know how to place buy/sell orders, and will become familiar and perfect about using your trading system. 2) You will gain confidence in yourself. 3) The fear of trading will vanish. It is very important to keep fear away while doing day trading. 4) You will become active to enter and exit the trade. It's vital important that you must be pretty fast to enter and exit the trade (i.e. open positions).

What are the common day trading mistakes and how to avoid them to make generous profit

1) Don't jump in trend early - Wait and get paper confirmation of trend change, and then plan and do your trades (buy/sell). Don't jump in or do early trades before any trade change

confirmation this may damage your capital (bank balance).

2) Don't wait in trade for long time - Suppose that you had done one trade (either buy or sell) but the scrip is not moving either up or down, it is just stable or moving with very low price difference, then you should get out of that trade and look for other scrip's. You may encounter these type of situations when indices (NSE or BSE) and not moving (or moving with narrow range). At such time either you wait or come out of trade, don't loose patience and fall under loss.

3) Don't change your trend on volume volatility - Some time you enter in trade by seeing the buy and sell quantities. For example, suppose you brought shares by seeing more buy quantity then sell quantity, expecting more buy quantity may push the share/stock up but after few minutes you see exactly reverse that you see more sell quantity and less buy quantity or both buy and sell high quantity or the difference of buying and selling quantity is decreased as compared

to what you had seen before. So this point is very important, don't panic here and sell off your stock, wait and realize the situation properly and then take action. This situation comes many times but if you are sure that your share is going to move up then stick to it.

4) Beware of companies' acquisition or any announcement by Government - Suppose in the morning, before market begins, you should read or viewed the news of any Indian Company has acquired any foreign company (or part of foreign company) if you see this is actually best news/things that Indian company. But if acquisition amount is far more than expectation then this good news will turn into worst news. The shares of that company will start falling. So you should not get in trade and buy shares you have to wait and watch how market or other people are responding to these shares and once you understand then you can trade. So always watch where the market heading towards and then react. Announcement of Government - You should also be very careful to decide your tarde based on any government

announcement. For example, if government has declared any hike in interest rate then its good news for bank stocks and hence the shares will rise but if government has declared 2nd rate hike in very less span of time as company to first one (stay within duration of one, two month or three month) then this news will be worse for bank stocks, the share may keeping fall during the trading period. So realize and analyze the news and finally watch market behavior and this fall or do trade you will get success.

Things to study in the morning before starting your day trading or share market trading or Intraday trading?

1) Read financial newspaper like Business Standard, Economics Times, etc. If possible note done the high lights/breaking news with respective company names and keep close watch on them for that day.

2) If possible watch share (stock) market related TV channels like Zee Business,

CNBC, etc. In these TV channels you get over all idea/movements of all share prices and markets (BSE, NSE). And also it becomes easy to catch and keep close watch on related companies if any breaking news comes out during that day.

3) Especially some share market related websites like capitalmarket.com, businessstandard.com always displays current news, market affairs, share market trends, breaking news and various announcement done by company or government which may effect the share market and related companies. So try to access and have all OK on such types of websites before starting trading and also through out the day, if possible.

4) So in short before starting you stock market trading you should be well aware of all the current news of financial market and if possible note down the breaking news or effective news and its related company and keep watch on that share and trade accordingly on that day.

Important principles to be follow by day tradersNever invest all your money in same sector this method is called as diversification of shares. This will protect your money from downtrends of any particular sector as you can make money from other sector.There are various sectors like IT, Pharmacy, Banking, Steel, Petrol and Oil, construction and infrastructure, auto etc.

Avoid common day trading mistakes Lack of a Trading Plan, Failure to Control Emotions, Failure to Accept and Limit Losses, Lack of Commitment, Over-Trading

How to Develop a Profitable Day Trading System

In this article I will explain to you how to develop a profitable day trading system in five steps:

Step 1: Select a market and a timeframe

Step 2: Define entry rules

Step 3: Define exit rules

Step 4: Evaluate your day trading system

Step 5: Improving the day trading system

Let's take a closer look at these steps.

Step 1: Select a market and a timeframe

Every market and every timeframe can be traded with a day trading system. But if you want to look at 50 different futures markets and 6 major timeframes (e.g. 5min, 10min, 15min, 30min, 60min and daily), then you need to evaluate 300 possible options. Here are some hints on how to limit your choices:

o Though you can trade every futures markets, we recommend that you stick to the electronic markets (e.g. e-mini S&P and other indices, Treasury Bonds and Notes, Currencies, etc). Usually these markets are very liquid, and you won't have a problem entering and exiting a trade. Another advantage of electronic markets is lower commissions: Expect to pay at least half the commissions you pay on non-electronic markets. Sometimes the difference can be as high as 75%.

o When you select a smaller timeframes (less than 60min) your average profit per trade is usually comparably low. On the other hand you get more trading opportunities. When trading on a larger timeframe your profits per trade will be bigger, but you will have less trading opportunities. It's up to you to decide which timeframe suits you best.

o Smaller timeframes mean smaller profits, but usually smaller risk, too. When you are starting with a small trading account, then you might want to select a small timeframe to make sure that you are not overtrading your account.

Most profitable day trading systems use larger timeframes like daily and weekly. These systems work, too, but, be prepared for less trading action and bigger drawdowns.

Step 2: Define entry rules

Let's simplify the myths of "entry rules":

Basically there are 2 different kinds of entry setups:

o Trend-following

When prices are moving up, you buy, and when prices are going down, you sell.

o Trend-fading

When prices are trading at an extreme (e.g. upper band of a channel), you sell, and you try to catch the small move while prices are moving back into "normalcy". The same applies for selling.

In my opinion swing trading is actually one of the best trading strategies for the beginning trader to get his or her feet wet. By contrast, trend trading offers greater profit potential if a trader is able to catch a major market trend of weeks or months, but few are the traders with sufficient discipline to hold a position for that period of time without getting distracted.

Most indicators that you will find in your charting software belong to one of these two categories: You have either indicators for identifying trends (e.g. Moving Averages) or indicators that define overbought or oversold situations and therefore offer you a trade setup for a short term swing trade.

So don't become confused by all the possibilities of entering a trade. Just make sure that you understand why you are using a certain indicator or what the indicator is measuring. An example of a simple swing daytrading strategy can be found in the next chapter.

Step 3: Define exit rules

Let's keep it simple here, too: There are two different exit rules you want to apply:

o Stop Loss Rules to protect your capital and

o Profit Taking Exits to realize your profits

Both exit rules can be expressed in four ways:

o A fixed dollar amount (e.g. $1,000)

o A percentage of the current price (e.g. 1% of the entry price)

o A percentage of the volatility (e.g. 50% of the average daily movement) or

o A time stop (e.g. exit after 3 days)

We don't recommend using a fixed dollar amount, because markets are too different. For example, natural gas changes an average of a few thousand dollars per day per contract; however, Eurodollars change an average of a few hundred dollars a day per contract. You need to balance and normalize this difference when developing a day trading system and testing it on different markets. That's why you should always use percentages for stops and profit targets (e.g. 1% stop) or a volatility stop instead of a fixed dollar amount.

A time stop gets you out of a trade if it is not moving in any direction, therefore freeing your capital for other trades.

Step 4: Evaluate your day trading system

The first figure to look for is the net profit. Obviously you want your system to generate profits. But don't be frustrated when during the development stage your day trading system shows a loss; try to reverse your entry signals. if you are going long at a certain price level, and you lose, then try to go short instead. Many times this is the easiest way to turn a losing system into a winning one.

The next figure you want to look at is the average profit per trade. Make sure this number is greater than slippage and commissions, and that it makes your day trading worthwhile. Day trading is all about risk and reward, and you want to make sure you get a decent reward for your risk.

Take a look at the Profit Factor (Gross Profit / Gross Loss). This will tell you how many dollars you are likely to win for every dollar you lose. The higher the profit factor the better the day trading system. A system should have a profit factor of 1.5 or more, but watch out when you see profit factors above 3.0, because it might be that you over-optimized the system.

Here are some more characteristics you might want to consider besides the net profit of a system:

o Winning percentage

Many profitable day trading systems achieve a nice net profit with a rather small winning percentage, sometimes even below 30%. These systems follow the principle "Cut your losses short and let your profits run". However, YOU need to decide whether you can stand 7 losers and only 3 winners in 10 trades. If you want to be "right" most of the time, then you should pick a system with a high winning percentage.

o Number of Trades per Month

Do you need daily action? If you want to see something happening every day, then you should pick a day trading system with a high number of trades per month. Many profitable day trading systems generate only 2-3 trades per month, but if you are not patient enough to wait for it, then you should select a day trading system with a higher trading frequency.

o Average Time in Trade

Some people get really nervous when they are in a trade. I have heard of people who can't even sleep at night when they have an open position. If that's you, then you should make sure that the average time in a trade is as short as possible. You might want to choose a system that does not hold any positions overnight.

o Maximum Drawdown

A famous trader once said: "If you want your system to double or triple your account, you should expect a drawdown of up to 30% on your way to trading riches." Not every trader can stand a 30% drawdown. Look at the maximum drawdown the system produced so far, and double it. If you can stand this drawdown, then you found the right day trading system. Why doubling? Remember: your worst drawdown is always ahead of you.

o Most consecutive losses

The amount of most consecutive losses has a huge impact on your trading, especially when you are using certain types of money management techniques. Five or six consecutive losses can cause you a lot of trouble when using an aggressive money management.

In addition this number will help you to determine whether you have enough discipline to trade the system: Will you still trade the system after you have experienced 10 losses in a row? It's not unusual for a profitable trading system to have 10-12 losses in a row.

Step 5: Improving your system

There is a difference between "improving" and "curve-fitting" a system. You can improve your day trading system by testing different exit methods: If you are using a fixed stop, try a trailing stop instead. Add a time stop and evaluate the results again. Don't look at the net profit only; look also at the profit factor, average profit per trade and maximum drawdown. Many times you will see that the net profit slightly decreases when you add different stops, but the other figures might improve dramatically.

Don't fall into the trap of over-optimizing: You can eliminate almost all losers by adding enough rules. Simple example: If you see that on Tuesdays you had more losers than on the other weekdays, you might be tempted to add a "filter" that prevents your day trading system from entering trades on Tuesdays. Next you find that in January you had much worse results than in other months, so you add a filter that enters trades only from February - December. You add more and more filters to avoid losses, and eventually you end up with a trading rule that I saw recently:

IF FVE > -1 And Regression Slope (Close , 35) / Close.35 * 100 > -.35 And Regression Slope (Close , 35) / Close.35 * 100 -.4 And Regression Slope (Close , 70) / Close.70 * 100 -.2 And MACD Diff (Close , 12 , 26 , 9) > -.003 And Not Tuesday And Not DayOfMonth = 12 and not Month = August and Time > 9:30 ...

Though you eliminated all possibilities of losing (in the past) and this trading system is now producing fantastic profits, it's very unlikely that it will continue to do so when it hits reality.

Day Trading Indicators and Indicator Trading

Did You Begin Day Trading As An Indicator Only Trader?

Did you start day trading after buying a book on technical analysis, and getting a charting program - probably a free one that you found online - in order to save money? While reading your book you learned about trading indicators which could 'predict' price movement, and what do you know, the 'best' indicators were actually included in your free charting program - let the games begin.

Now that you have all the day trading tools that are necessary, the book for education AND the free charting program with those 'best' day trading indicators, you now need a day trading plan so you can decide which ones of those 'magic' day trading indicators you are supposed to use. This really is a great book, besides telling you how to day trade using indicators to 'predict' price - it also said that you need a trading plan to day trade.

So what should this plan be? The book told you about trend following using an indicator called macd, and it also told you how it was possible to pick the top or bottoms using an indicator called stochastic; my guess is that you picked the stochastic indicator to start your day trading - this must be the 'best of the best' since this indicator was going to ensure you of entering your trades with the 'best' price. Amazing, simply amazing how easy this day trading stuff really is. In fact, why even bother taking the trades, each time your indicators give a signal - just call up your broker and tell him to stick $100 in your account.

My book was Technical Analysis of the Futures Markets. My charting program was TradeStation with an eSignal fm receiver; that was the one that if you hung the antennae wires just right, and you put enough foil on the tips, you might even get quotes. I had sold a business before I started trading so I did have some capital

- isn't that how everyone gets into trading, you either sell a business or you lose your job? My indicator was the macd as I had decided that I was going to be a 'trend follower' instead of a 'top-bottom picker'. I also decided that I was going to be 'extra' clever, if one indicator was good than two indicators must be better, so I added a 20 period moving average. My first trade was a winner, then after many months of extensive therapy, I was finally able to forget the next twelve months - ahhh the memories J

Learning To Day Trading - The Learning Progression

Beginning to day trade, or learning to day trade, as an indicator trader is very typical. This is also logical when you consider - HOW are you supposed to initially learn how to trade? Trading indicators are available to anyone who has a charting program, and simply using line crosses, or histogram color changes, provide 'easy' signals to understand. If you will also take the time to learn the arithmetic behind your indicators, as well as learning what each indicator is specifically intended to do, not only is this a logical way to begin, it is also a good 'step' in your learning progression - understanding the WHAT you are doing, instead of attempting to create 'canned' indicator only trading systems, without any regard as to WHY you are trading this way.

This does become one of the 'sticking' points in your learning progression, as you come to find out that you are unable to profitably trade indicators as signals only - now what? Now what - you 'can't' develop your own indicators, so you start doing Google searches for day trading indicators and start buying your 'collection' - they don't 'work' either. Now what - you buy a mechanical trading system - what does hypothetical results may not be indicative of real trading or future results mean? Now what - you start subscribing to signal services OR you start joining the 'latest and greatest' chat room - am I really the only person using the signals who isn't profitable?

Now what - you never learn how to trade.

I began trading as an indicator trader, and I did try to learn everything that I could about the various indicators, as well as trying to combine indicators that were consistent with how I wanted to trade - I just could never develop a mechanical day trading system from what was available to me. I read a couple more books that didn't really help me, so I then started looking for someone who could teach me. From what I now know about gurus -vs- teachers, I am very lucky that I got involved with a money manager-trader who taught me a tremendous amount, but I still couldn't get profitable, in part because there was also 'pressure' to learn how to trade using real money. As well, any discussions or thoughts about trading psychology and the issues involved, especially to beginning traders, was non-existent.

Now what - learning but losing - I stopped trading.

Learning to trading using real money, and 'scoffing' at trading psychology as simply individual weakness, really was something that I now regard as misinformation. I always mention this as I now feel that this cost me as much as a year of time, and was very close to costing me my trading future, as stopped trading was VERY close to quitting trading. How can't trading psychology be real to a beginner, when you consider that you are risking losing money at a very fast pace as a day trader, and when you further consider that you are also doing this when you really don't know what you are doing - this is NOT by definition being weak. And if trading psychology is real, how are you going to learn to make 'good' trading habits with real money while you are fighting the implications?

Now what - not trading and not ready [quite] to quit - still studying and searching.

Probably the single most important 'thing' that got me to a next step in learning how to trade, was the concept of a trading setup, and that a setup and a signal were not the same. This was extremely meaningful to me, as it also led to an understanding of how to better use trading indicators for the information that they can provide, but not to use them as trading signals - in essence I began learning about trading method where discretion could be consistently applied - vs- trading system that was mechanical and arithmetic rules.

Traders who are indicator only traders, are also what I refer to right side only traders, that is they are always looking at the right side of their charts for an indicator signal. BUT what about the left side of the chart, what about price and patterns, what about market conditions - WHAT about the relevant 'things' that are 'moving' price, instead of indicators only as an arithmetic derivative of price, and thus, one that is dependent on the time frame that you have chosen to trade from? These 'thoughts', along with the concept of trade setup, became instrumental in the development of a trading method, and how I came to turning my trading around.

When I think about the steps in my learning progression - I would list them as follows:

2/95 - 6/96

indicators only

teaching service that included signals

learning to trading with real money and trading psychology issues

stop trading

6/96 - 3/97

understanding of trading psychology issues

learning about trading setups concept

trading method -vs- trading system

trade setup - trade trigger are not the same

method development

understand the importance of the left side of the chart and what is happening 'across' the chart

related trading setups and how/when they triggered

indicators + pattern

indicators + pattern + price

indicators + pattern + price + market conditions

3/97 - 11/97

able to paper trade profitably

able to real money trade profitably

able to trade for a living

Indicator Only Day Trader - Setup Including Indicators Method Day Trader

I have attempted to discuss the way I started day trading, and the way I think many-most traders typically begin. Along with this, I have pointed various issues and problems that I had - those regarding how to learn to trade, and then progressing into a profitable trader. My experiences have been both personal, as well as those of many traders that I have worked with over the last 8-9 years through Tactical Trading - that a very large number of these problems are due to day trading only with indicators, the specific indicators used, along with trying to turn these indicators into a mechanical trading system. This is not to say that this can't be done - I simply couldn't do it. However, I would strongly suggest that anyone who is in the early stages of day trading, or struggling with their day trading, consider these things that have been discussed.

Conclusion

Thank you again for downloading this book!

I hope this book was able to help you to UNDERSTAND how to utilize the opportunity of DAY TRADING. Keep learning and improve more.

Finally, if you enjoyed this book, then I'd like to ask you for a favor, would you be kind enough to leave a review for this book on Amazon? It'd be greatly appreciated!

Thank you and good luck!

I truly do appreciate it!

Best Wishes,

Lee Maxwell

www.ingramcontent.com/pod-product-compliance
Lightning Source LLC
Chambersburg PA
CBHW070107210526
45170CB00013B/776